COWBOY
COOK BOOK

Great Recipes
from Cowboy Country!

by
Bruce & Bobbi Fischer

Photo on front and back covers: Robert Dawson/Adstock

Other books by Bruce and Bobbi Fischer:

Tortilla Lovers Cook Book
Grand Canyon Cook Book
Western Breakfast and Brunch Recipes
Utah Cook Book

Acknowledgements

We are grateful to all the kind folks who have contributed their tried-and-true recipes:

Karen May, North Fork Guest Ranch, Shawnee, Colorado; Sharon Blixrud, Seven Lazy P Guest Ranch, Choteau, Montana; Stephanie Zier, Spear-O-Wigwam Ranch, Sheridan, Wyoming; Jimmy B. Combs, Diamond J Ranch, Ennis, Montana; Roxann Van Orden, Moose Creek Ranch, Victor, Idaho; June Voldseth, Bonanza Creek Country, Martensdale, Montana; Billie Garnick, Triangle C Ranch, Dubois, Wyoming; Brent Ewald, Hargrave Cattle and Guest Ranch, Marion, Montana; Diana Swift Bryant, Wapiti Meadow Ranch, Cascade, Idaho; Todd Scott, Lazy K-Bar Ranch, Tucson, Arizona.

Selected cowboy sayings from *Cowboy Slang* by Edgar R. "Frosty" Potter and Stella Hughes quote (p. 6) from *Arizona Territory Cook Book* courtesy of Golden West Publishers.

Printed in the United States Of America

ISBN 13: 978-1-885590-96-1
ISBN 10: 1-885590-96-2
5th Printing © 2007

Golden West Publishers
4113 N. Longview
Phoenix, AZ 85014
(800) 658-5830

For sample recipes for every Golden West cookbook, visit: www.goldenwestpublishers.com

Cowboy
Cook Book
Table of Contents

Main Dishes

Side Dishes

Table of Contents (continued)

Introduction

Food was arguably the most important thing to cowboys on the range. Although cowboys were well paid, they always wanted to know what kind of "chuck," or food, was served on the trail before they signed onto a "wagon," or crew. In effect, it was the chuck wagon cook, not the money, that made a cowboy's hardships endurable.

And so the chuck wagon cook determined the success or failure of a roundup based on the quality of food he set in front of the cowboys. Consequently, trail cooks were the most important members of the crew and were paid twice as much as cowboys. Cookie worked hard for his wages, though. He rose at three every morning before any cowboy to start coffee and breakfast, dug five-foot deep barbeque pits and three-foot deep beanholes, loaded and unloaded the wagon and hauled around the cast iron Dutch ovens.

Cowgirl and experienced ranch cook Stella Hughes of Arizona knows firsthand about this grueling, most important roundup role. Offering her authentic take on the trail cook's job, she said, "Oh, I was on standby in case the cook quit . . . but I drove the cattle all the way and said fervent prayers each day that the cook stayed until the drive was over. Truly, there is no harder job than slinging heavy Dutch ovens and preparing meals for 20 men over an open fire."

Thanks to those in the acknowledgments, recipes in this book reflect both old and new versions of cowboy cooking. Just as the desert landscape has shifted since the days of the Ol' West, so, too, have cowboys' ways shifted. These recipes do not necessarily reflect old ranch-style methods of cooking. There are no instructions on how to dig a beanhole or barbecue pit, and no specific advice is given about cooking over a campfire. Instead, these recipes call for modern cooking methods. Many ingredients that cowboys would not have had access to in the 1800s are called for in these recipes so that they appeal to today's tastes. As a result, everyone, from the roughest ranch hands to citified buckaroos, can enjoy these recipes.

Breakfasts & Beverages

Cookie is King!

Cowboys walked delicately around Cookie; no one dared to cross him! As the sayin' goes, "Cussin' a range cook is as risky as brandin' a mule's tail!" During the roundup, Cookie always made sure he had a jug of sourdough to make hoecakes and flapjacks. Flapjacks were similar to pancakes only larger and thicker. With a flick of the range cook's wrist, the flapjack was turned and browned to perfection! Hungry cowboys lined up, waiting to feast upon this delicacy.

Hearty Sourdough Pancakes

For crunchy pancakes, substitute 1 cup of granola for the brown sugar in this recipe. A cup of blueberries or other fruit added just before cooking is another favorite variation.

2 cups SOURDOUGH STARTER (see pg. 69)
2 EGGS
2 tsp. BROWN SUGAR

1/4 cup DRY MILK
FLOUR
WATER
1 tsp. BAKING SODA

Mix sourdough starter, eggs, sugar and dry milk. If mixture is too thin, add flour to desired consistency. If mixture is too thick, add water. Stir in baking soda and allow to stand for 1 minute. Ladle or pour batter onto a greased skillet (cast iron works best). Fry until bubbles form and break on top. Turn and continue frying until golden brown.

Sourdough Saddles Up

No cowboy's meal was complete without sourdough. In fact, the sourdough starter–generally stored in a wooden keg or crock–had some uncanny things in common with cowboys themselves: it required regular feeding, improved with age, needed to be kept warm on chilly nights and wasn't disturbed traveling over rough terrain.

Panhandler Pancakes

4 EGGS, separated
1 cup COTTAGE CHEESE,
   creamed

1/4 cup FLOUR
1/2 tsp. SALT

Beat egg whites until stiff, but not dry. Beat yolks with electric mixer until light in color. Stir cottage cheese, flour and salt into egg yolks; gently fold in egg whites until thoroughly combined. Cook on a well-greased griddle.

Makes 8 (5-inch) pancakes.

Eggs on a Shell

6 TOSTADA SHELLS
1 can (7 oz.) MEXICAN TOMATO SAUCE
2 Tbsp. chopped GREEN ONIONS
2 cloves GARLIC, minced
1 TOMATO, diced
CAYENNE to taste
6 EGGS
1 cup grated MONTEREY JACK CHEESE

Heat tostada shells in a 250° oven until warm. In a saucepan, combine red sauce, green onions, garlic, tomato and cayenne; bring to a boil; reduce heat and let simmer. Arrange tostada shells on a baking sheet. Fry eggs over easy and place one on each tostada shell. Spoon sauce over eggs and top with cheese. Place under the broiler until cheese melts and is bubbly; serve immediately.

Cowboy's Oats

When you live on a ranch, the days start early! The chores have to be done; even the animals are fed before you! So when breakfast finally comes, you've got a big appetite.

8 cups ROLLED OATS
1/3 cup CORN OIL
2/3 cup HONEY
1 cup chopped ALMONDS
1 cup RAISINS
1 cup chopped DATES
3/4 cup WHEAT GERM

Spread oats on the surface of a lightly greased cookie sheet and bake at 350° for 10 minutes. In a bowl, mix baked oats, oil, honey and almonds together. Spread mixture in a 13 x 9 pan and return to oven for 30 minutes; stir every 10 minutes. Remove from oven and cool. Combine with raisins, dates and wheat germ. Mix well and store in the refrigerator. Serve with warm milk.

The chuck wagon cook called the cowboys to eat in a variety of colorful ways, including:

- *Grab a plate an' growl*
- *Grab it now, or I'll spit in the skillet*
- *Grub pile, come a-runnin' fellers*
- *Chuck away, come an' get it*

Apple Pecan Pancakes

3 APPLES, peeled and diced
1/2 cup chopped PECANS
1/2 cup SUGAR
3 tsp. CINNAMON
1/4 cup WATER
4 cups FLOUR
5 tsp. BAKING POWDER
1 tsp. SALT
1 tsp. NUTMEG
4 EGGS, beaten
2/3 cup packed BROWN SUGAR
2 tsp. VANILLA
4 cups HALF AND HALF
1/2 cup BUTTER, melted and cooled

Place apples in a microwavable bowl with pecans, sugar, 2 teaspoons cinnamon and water. Mix well and microwave on high for about 4-5 minutes. Set aside. In a large bowl, mix flour, baking powder, salt, remaining cinnamon and nutmeg. In a separate bowl, mix together eggs, brown sugar, vanilla and half and half, whisking well while adding. Slowly add melted butter to egg mixture. Add the liquid ingredients to the dry ingredients and thoroughly blend; add apple mixture and mix well. Spoon onto hot greased griddle and cook until bubbles form; flip and cook to desired doneness.

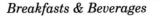
Three Cheese Egg Bake

"This easy casserole can be prepared, refrigerated overnight and then baked for an early breakfast."

4 EGGS
1/2 cup WHIPPING CREAM
1 tsp. SUGAR
1/2 lb. MONTEREY JACK CHEESE, shredded
2 oz. CREAM CHEESE, cubed
1 cup COTTAGE CHEESE
3 Tbsp. BUTTER
1/4 cup chopped GREEN ONIONS
1/2 cup FLOUR
1 tsp. BAKING POWDER

In a bowl, beat eggs, whipping cream and sugar together. Stir in the cheeses and mix well. Melt butter in a small skillet and lightly sauté green onions; stir in flour and baking powder. Combine mixtures and blend well. Pour batter into a greased 1 1/2-quart casserole dish and bake at 325° for 45 minutes (if refrigerated, bake for 1 hour).

Mr. Everything!
Cowboy cooks not only cooked three meals a day, they also served as the camp doctor, dentist, barber, counselor and peacemaker!

Sunflower Oat Breakfast Crunch

This can be served as a great breakfast cereal or used as a high-energy trail mix.

5 cups OATS
3/4 cup SALAD OIL
1 cup slivered ALMONDS
3/4 cup HONEY
1 cup SHREDDED COCONUT
1 cup WHEAT GERM

1/2 cup WATER
1/2 Tbsp. SALT
1 Tbsp. VANILLA
1 cup SUNFLOWER
  SEEDS

In a large bowl, mix all ingredients together and spread in a jelly roll pan. Toast in a 300° oven for 30 minutes. Stir at least every 10 minutes. Let cool and place in a plastic container or bag. Refrigerate.

Ranch-Style Eggs

1/4 cup OIL
4 CORN TORTILLAS
8 EGGS
GREEN CHILE SAUCE
1 cup grated CHEDDAR CHEESE

In a skillet over medium heat, add oil and heat tortillas for 1 minute each. Drain on paper towels. Poach eggs. Set two poached eggs on each tortilla; top with green chile sauce to taste. Sprinkle with grated cheese. Place under broiler for a few minutes until cheese is melted.

Texas-Style Granola

2 1/2 cups ROLLED OATS
1 cup SHREDDED COCONUT
1/2 cup WHEAT GERM
1/2 cup SESAME SEEDS
1/2 cup chopped ALMONDS
1/2 cup shelled SUNFLOWER SEEDS
1/2 cup HONEY
1/2 cup SALAD OIL
1/2 cup chopped DATES
1/2 cup RAISINS

In a large mixing bowl, combine oats, coconut, wheat germ, sesame seeds, almonds and sunflower seeds. Mix thoroughly. Add honey and oil; mix until oat mixture is thoroughly coated. Spread mixture in a 13 x 9 baking pan and bake at 250° for 45 minutes. Stir every 15 minutes. Remove from the oven and stir in dates and raisins. Allow mixture to cool, stirring occasionally to keep from sticking. Once cooled, place granola in a plastic container and refrigerate until ready to use.

Cowboy Fast Food

On the trail, cowboys carried foods like jerky, nuts, dried fruit and biscuits or hard tack. A favorite snack was pemmican (cakes made from a thick paste of ground dried meat or fish mixed with hot fat and dried berries).

Maple Syrup Soufflé

1 1/2 cups MAPLE SYRUP
4 EGG WHITES
2 tsp. BAKING POWDER
1/2 cup SUGAR

3 Tbsp. COGNAC
1 Tbsp. BUTTER,
melted

In a saucepan, boil 1 cup of maple syrup until it is reduced to 3/4 cup. Allow to cool. In a bowl, beat egg whites and 2 tablspoons sugar until stiff peaks form. Fold baking powder and remaining sugar into egg whites, mixing well. Gently fold cooled maple syrup into egg mixture. Place remaining maple syrup in an 8-inch soufflé pan and stir in cognac and butter. Pour egg mixture on top. Put soufflé pan in pan of warm water and bake for 1 hour at 300°. Serve with maple syrup on the side.

Bar-B French Toast

8 slices (1-inch thick)
FRENCH BREAD
8 tsp. APRICOT JAM
4 lg. EGGS

1 cup MILK
1 tsp. VANILLA
1 Tbsp. BUTTER
POWDERED SUGAR

With a serrated knife, cut a pocket into each slice of bread to within 1/4 inch of the crust. Spread 1 teaspoon jam in each pocket; seal. In a shallow bowl, combine eggs, milk and vanilla; beat well. Dip bread into egg mixture until well saturated. In a skillet, melt butter and cook bread slices until golden brown. Turn and brown the other side. Sprinkle with powdered sugar and serve.

Hash Brown & Egg Burritos

12 (10-inch) FLOUR TORTILLAS
1/4 cup BUTTER or MARGARINE
1 pkg. (24 oz.) frozen HASH BROWNS
10 EGGS, beaten
1-2 cups grated CHEDDAR CHEESE
1 can (4 oz.) DICED GREEN CHILES, drained
1 cup PICANTE SAUCE
1 cup chopped GREEN ONIONS

Wrap tortillas in foil and place in a 250° oven to warm. Melt butter in a large skillet; add hash browns and cook according to package directions. When browned, reduce heat to medium. Stir in eggs and cook until eggs are lightly scrambled and set. Unwrap tortillas and place on serving dishes. Top each tortilla with 1/2 cup of the hash brown and egg mixture; add cheese, chiles, picante sauce and green onions, as desired. Roll up tortillas and serve.

Blueberry Coffee Cake

3/4 cup SUGAR	1 tsp. BAKING POWDER
1/2 cup UNSALTED	1 tsp. BAKING SODA
BUTTER, softened	1/8 tsp. SALT
1/2 tsp. VANILLA	1 1/4 cups SOUR CREAM
3 EGGS	1 cup BLUEBERRIES
2 cups WHITE FLOUR	

Preheat oven to 350°. Grease and flour a 13 x 9 baking pan. In a bowl, cream together sugar and butter with an electric mixer. Add vanilla and eggs and beat on low speed until smooth. In a separate bowl, sift together flour, baking powder, baking soda and salt. Alternately add small portions of dry ingredients and sour cream to egg mixture. Beat for 1 minute at medium speed. Gently stir in blueberries. Spread batter in prepared baking pan. Sprinkle *Walnut Pecan Topping* evenly over the batter and bake for 30-45 minutes or until a toothpick inserted in the center comes out clean.

Walnut Pecan Topping

1 1/4 cup SUGAR	2 tsp. CINNAMON
1/2 cup chopped WALNUTS	3 Tbsp. BUTTER,
1/2 cup chopped PECANS	melted

In a bowl, combine sugar, walnuts, pecans and cinnamon. Stir in butter and blend well.

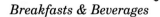

Cowboys & Their Coffee

Cowboys loved their coffee; having their coffee was as important as having a wide-brimmed hat, a saddle and a horse!

Usually cowboys put ground coffee in the coffeepot with cold water, brought the coffee to a boil, then settled it with a bit more water. And if they found themselves without a coffeepot, they boiled the grounds in the same frying pan they had just cooked their bacon in!

Cowboys called coffee "java," and they sweetened it with sorghum molasses if a Southern cowboy and cane sugar if a Northerner.

Cowboys had a knack for describing their favorite beverage. Some reportedly said, "The coffee tasted like water scalded to death." Others claimed the "coffee was made out of water thick enough to plow," or the "coffee was so thick yuh had to use sandpaper to get the settlin's out of yore mouth."

Some exclaimed, "He likes coffee that'll kick up in the middle an' pack double" or "His coffee was thick 'nough to eat with a fork." Others stated "The coffee was strong 'nough to haul a wagon!"

Cowboy Coffee

4 qts. WATER
1 1/2 cups freshly-ground
COFFEE

1 EGG SHELL
1/2 cup COLD WATER

Bring water to a boil in a large saucepan. Add coffee and egg shell to boiling water. Return to a boil; remove from heat and let stand for 2 minutes. Slowly add cold water to settle grounds to the bottom. Strain if desired.

Mexican Coffee

12 cups hot, strong BLACK COFFEE
1 1/2 oz. UNSWEETENED CHOCOLATE
1/2 cup packed LIGHT BROWN SUGAR
1/2 cup SUGAR
1/2 tsp. CINNAMON
1/2 cup COFFEE LIQUEUR
WHIPPED CREAM

Pour coffee into a large saucepan. Add chocolate, sugars, cinnamon and liqueur. Stir over moderate heat until chocolate is melted. Serve in heated cups; top with whipped cream.

Sweet Coffee

3 cups COFFEE
3 cups HALF AND HALF
1/2 cup CRÈME DE CACAO

1/4 cup RUM
1/4 cup BRANDY

Combine all ingredients in a saucepan and heat thoroughly. Serve immediately.

Hot Spiced Wine

4 cups WATER
2 cups SUGAR
1 tsp. WHOLE CLOVES
6 CINNAMON STICKS
3 LEMONS, thinly sliced
1/2 cup APRICOT BRANDY
1/2 gal. BURGUNDY WINE

Combine water, sugar, cloves, and cinnamon sticks in a large heavy saucepan; boil for 5 minutes. Remove from heat and add lemons. Stir and allow to stand for 20 minutes. Remove cloves and cinnamon sticks; add brandy and wine. Return to heat; simmer until very hot. Serve in mugs.

Orange Clove Tea

1/3 cup SUGAR
3 TEA BAGS
12 WHOLE CLOVES
1 CINNAMON STICK
1 (4-inch) strip fresh ORANGE PEEL
3 cups BOILING WATER
1/2 cup freshly-squeezed ORANGE JUICE
3 Tbsp. LEMON JUICE
LEMON SLICES, studded with WHOLE CLOVES

Place sugar, tea bags, cloves, cinnamon and orange peel in a saucepan and pour boiling water over top. Steep for 5 minutes; strain. Pour tea back into saucepan and stir in orange and lemon juices. Heat, but do not boil. Serve in cups garnished with lemon slices.

Salads, Soups, Stews & Chowders

The Chuck Wagon

The chuck wagon was invented by Texas cattle-man Charles Goodnight in 1866 before his first cattle drive fom Texas to the Kansas railroad. A tall chuck box was nailed on the back of a wagon, and its door dropped down to make a table. Shelves and drawers inside the box let the potwrangler store everything he needed, from his sourdough keg to tin plates, cups and eating irons.

The chuck wagon was the hub of cowboy life. It was around the chuck wagon that they ate, told stories, sang songs, gossiped, talked over the day's events and just plain relaxed before heading for their bedrolls.

Steak House Salad

Dressing:
   3/4 cup VINEGAR
   3/4 cup SUGAR
   1/2 cup OIL
   1 tsp. SALT
   1 tsp. PEPPER

2 cans (15.25 oz. ea.) CORN, drained
1 can (15 oz.) PETITE PEAS, drained
1 can (14 oz.) GREEN BEANS, drained
1 jar (4 oz.) DICED PIMENTOS
1 ONION, chopped or 1 bunch GREEN
      ONIONS, sliced
1 GREEN BELL PEPPER, chopped

In a saucepan, combine dressing ingredients and bring to a boil. Simmer for 10 minutes; cool. Place remaining ingredients in a bowl and toss. Pour cooled dressing over vegetables and refrigerate overnight. Stir well before serving.

Cowboy Etiquette
- *Don't let the pot lid touch the dirt*
- *Stand and ride downwind so you don't kick dust into the food*
- *Don't tie your horse to the chuck wagon*
- *Don't help yourself to cook's provisions*

Chopper Salad

Dressing:
   1/2 cup MAYONNAISE
   1 Tbsp. VINEGAR
   1/4 cup SUGAR

Salad:
   2-3 cups chopped fresh BROCCOLI
   2 cups chopped fresh CAULIFLOWER
   2/3 cup RAISINS
   1/2 cup SUNFLOWER SEEDS
   10 slices BACON, cooked and crumbled
   1 RED ONION, chopped

In a glass or ceramic bowl, combine all dressing ingredients; cover and refrigerate overnight. When ready to serve, place all salad ingredients in a large bowl; add dressing and toss.

Slim's Coleslaw

1 cup MAYONNAISE
2 Tbsp. VINEGAR
1 tsp. SALT
1/2 tsp. SUGAR
1/2 tsp. ground BLACK
   PEPPER

1/2 tsp. grated ONION
1 med. CABBAGE,
   shredded
2 CARROTS, shredded
1/4 GREEN BELL PEPPER,
   shredded

In a glass or ceramic bowl, combine mayonnaise and vinegar and stir until well blended. Add salt, sugar, black pepper and onion; mix thoroughly. Cover and refrigerate. When ready to serve, combine cabbage, carrots and bell pepper in a bowl; add mayonnaise mixture and toss until vegetables are well coated.

Easy Potato Salad

7 med. POTATOES, cooked in jackets, peeled
**   and sliced**
1/3 cup VINAIGRETTE
3/4 cup sliced CELERY
1/3 cup sliced GREEN ONIONS
4 HARD-BOILED EGGS
1 cup MAYONNAISE
1/2 cup SOUR CREAM
1 1/2 tsp. prepared HORSERADISH
SALT to taste
CELERY SEED to taste
1/3 cup diced CUCUMBER

While potatoes are still warm, place in a bowl and pour vinaigrette over top; chill for 2 hours. Combine celery and green onions with potatoes. Chop egg whites and add to potato mixture. In a bowl, mash egg yolks, reserving 1/4 cup for garnish. Combine yolks with mayonnaise, sour cream and horseradish. Fold into potato mixture. Add salt and celery seed. Cover and chill for at least 2 hours. Just before serving, stir in cucumber and sprinkle reserved yolk over top.

Cattle Brands

Cattlemen branded their cattle so that they would know which ones were theirs. Here are some brands the cowboys might have seen.

Flying D	7-Up	Rising Sun	Rocking Chair	Flying X	Keystone	Turkey Track	Broken Arrow

---

Chunky Potato Salad

4 med. POTATOES
1/2 cup chopped CELERY
1/3 cup chopped ONION
3/4 cup MAYONNAISE

1/4 cup MILK
1 tsp. SALT
1/4 tsp. PEPPER
1 Tbsp. PARSLEY

Peel potatoes, cut into halves and place in a saucepan; cover with water. Bring to a boil; cover and lower heat. Simmer for 20 minutes or until potatoes are tender; drain and cut into chunks. Combine remaining ingredients in a salad bowl; add potatoes and mix well. Chill before serving.

Garbanzo Bean Salad

1 can (16 oz.) GARBANZO BEANS, drained
20 BLACK OLIVES, sliced
1/2 cup chopped GREEN ONIONS
1 Tbsp. WORCESTERSHIRE SAUCE
1/2 cup VEGETABLE OIL
1/2 cup VINEGAR
SALT and PEPPER to taste

In a bowl, combine all ingredients and mix well. Cover and refrigerate at least 8 hours before serving.

Macaroni & Bacon Salad

Salad:
   1 pkg. (16 oz.) SMALL SHELL MACARONI
   1 bunch GREEN ONIONS, sliced
   1 jar (4 oz.) PIMENTOS
   1 can (2.25 oz.) SLICED BLACK OLIVES
   1 lb. BACON, cooked and crumbled
   2/3 cup sliced CELERY
   6 HARD-BOILED EGGS, chopped

Dressing:
   1/2 can (10.75 oz.) TOMATO SOUP
   1/2 cup MAYONNAISE
   1 Tbsp. WORCESTERSHIRE SAUCE
   1/2 Tbsp. HORSERADISH

Prepare macaroni according to package directions. Drain and rinse well. Place macaroni in a large bowl and add remaining salad ingredients; toss together. In a bowl, whisk together all dressing ingredients. Pour dressing over salad and toss. Cover and chill before serving.

The Wild, Wild West

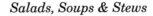

Buffalo Bill's Wild West Show took cowboys to cities and towns where people were not familiar with that lifestyle. Europeans were also very interested in the shows and, as a result, often perceived America as a wild western country.

Poppy Seed Dressing

Drizzle over fruit salads, shredded cabbage or avocado slices for a delicious treat.

1 1/2 cups SUGAR
2 tsp. DRY MUSTARD
2 tsp. SALT
2/3 cup WHITE VINEGAR
2 Tbsp. fresh ONION JUICE
2 cups VEGETABLE OIL
3 Tbsp. POPPY SEEDS

Combine sugar, mustard, salt and vinegar with an electric mixer. Add onion juice and mix well. Add vegetable oil slowly, beating constantly until mixture thickens. Add poppy seeds and beat two minutes longer. Cover and refrigerate.

Son-of-a-Gun Stew

Cowboys would look forward to when Cookie would make son-of-a-gun stew (it's name in polite company). Every cut of meat went into this specialty, including various organs such as liver, heart, sweetbreads and brain. The concoction was seasoned with onions and chiles and thickened with flour to create a unique trail experience.

Tumbling T's Stew

1 1/2 lbs. STEW MEAT,
   cut into 1-inch cubes
1 BAY LEAF
4 ONIONS, diced
4 med. RED POTATOES,
   cubed

6 CARROTS, sliced
2 Tbsp. PAPRIKA
SALT and PEPPER
4 Tbsp. FLOUR
1 cup COLD WATER

In a heavy skillet, cook meat until well browned; cover with water and simmer until tender. Add bay leaf, onions, potatoes, carrots and paprika; season with salt and pepper to taste. Mix flour and water to a smooth paste; add to stew, stirring constantly. Simmer until thickened and heated through.

Cowboy-Style Corn Chowder

1 slice BACON, chopped
1/8 cup sliced ONION
2 POTATOES, diced
1/4 tsp. CELERY SALT
1/2 tsp. PEPPER

1 cup WATER
1 1/2 cups CREAM
   STYLE CORN
2 cups MILK

In a skillet, cook bacon. Add onion and sauté until tender; set aside. In a saucepan, combine potatoes, celery salt, pepper and water. Bring to a boil and cook until potatoes are tender. Add corn, milk and bacon mixture to saucepan. Simmer until heated through.

Cattle Call Stew

2 lbs. BEEF STEW MEAT, cubed
2 ONIONS, diced
2 Tbsp. VEGETABLE OIL
2 1/2 cups HOT WATER
1 Tbsp. SUGAR
1/2 tsp. SALT
1 1/2 tsp. BLACK PEPPER
1 can (16 oz.) WHOLE TOMATOES,
    undrained
1 can (6 oz.) TOMATO PASTE
1 can (4.5 oz.) sliced MUSHROOMS
1 cup thinly sliced CARROTS
2 stalks CELERY, sliced
1/2 tsp. THYME
1/4 tsp. MARJORAM
1 BAY LEAF
2 Tbsp. FLOUR
1/4 cup COLD WATER

In a Dutch oven or large kettle, cook beef and onions in oil, stirring often, until meat is browned on all sides. Stir in hot water, sugar, salt, pepper, tomatoes, tomato paste and mushrooms. Heat to boiling, stirring occasionally. Reduce heat; cover and simmer, stirring occasionally, until beef is almost tender, about 1 1/2 hours. Add carrots, celery, thyme, marjoram and bay leaf. Cover and simmer for 30 minutes until vegetables are tender. Remove bay leaf. In a cup, mix flour and cold water; add to stew and stir until stew is thick and bubbly.

Mashed Potato Soup

8 POTATOES, peeled and cut into 1-inch pieces	1 ONION, diced
1/2 tsp. SALT	1 stalk CELERY, diced
2 Tbsp. BUTTER	8 MUSHROOMS, diced
1/2 cup MILK	1 qt. CHICKEN STOCK
2 Tbsp. OIL	1 tsp. MARJORAM
2 lg. CARROTS, diced	SALT and PEPPER to taste

In a large pot, cover potatoes with water and bring to a boil; simmer until tender. Remove from heat, drain and place in a mixing bowl. Add salt and butter and stir. Add milk and mash potatoes until smooth; set aside. Add oil to a skillet and sauté carrots, onion and celery until tender. Add mushrooms and sauté until tender. Place vegetables in a Dutch oven or large kettle; add chicken stock and marjoram. Bring mixture to a boil; reduce heat and simmer for 5 minutes. Blend in mashed potatoes, salt and pepper.

Did Cookie Fall Off the Horse or the Wagon?

The trail cook was often a former cowboy who could no longer ride and wrangle. Contrary to popular opinion, he was no more given to drinking than any other trail hand. His reputed grouchiness was likely a result of having to cook satisfying food under the most adverse conditions using the same ingredients every day.

Lazy Man's Stew

3 Tbsp. VEGETABLE OIL
3 ONIONS, sliced
2 lbs. BEEF, cut into chunks
3 Tbsp. FLOUR
2 tsp. SALT
1/4 tsp. PEPPER
1/4 tsp. THYME
1 cup CIDER
1 Tbsp. KETCHUP
3 POTATOES, peeled and quartered
4 CARROTS, peeled and sliced
4 Tbsp. FLOUR
1 cup COLD WATER

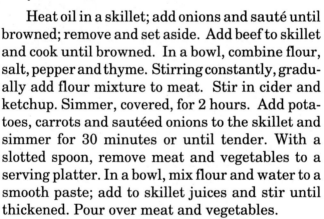

Heat oil in a skillet; add onions and sauté until browned; remove and set aside. Add beef to skillet and cook until browned. In a bowl, combine flour, salt, pepper and thyme. Stirring constantly, gradually add flour mixture to meat. Stir in cider and ketchup. Simmer, covered, for 2 hours. Add potatoes, carrots and sautéed onions to the skillet and simmer for 30 minutes or until tender. With a slotted spoon, remove meat and vegetables to a serving platter. In a bowl, mix flour and water to a smooth paste; add to skillet juices and stir until thickened. Pour over meat and vegetables.

Nothing Fancy
Cowboy fare mainly consisted of beef, beans, coffee, molasses, dried fruits, sourdough, potatoes, onions and canned veggies. Most foods were cooked in lard and seasoned with salt and pepper.

Main Dishes

Dutch Ovens

Some say the Dutch oven was invented in colonial times by Paul Revere. Whether this rarefied legend is true or not is unknown. What is known is this cast iron cooking utensil was one of the most useful items to folks on the frontier–"worth it's weight in gold."

It is not certain how the Dutch oven got its name. During colonial times, they were manufactured in the New England states, but after traders from Holland bought large quantities of these kettles to trade with those moving West, they grew in popularity until the sturdy yet portable ovens were considered a frontier necessity. Some think that the Dutch oven was named after the Dutch traders who were peddling it. Others believe that the name refers to the Dutch metal-casting process that was used to manufacture these pots. And there are some who maintain that the name is associated with the Pennsylvania Dutch who used a similar type of cast iron kettle. However it may have acquired its name, the name stuck. "Dutch oven" it remains.

Dutch ovens should be seasoned like cast iron skillets. They function like skillets or pots when they are sitting on top of the coals, but they work like ovens when coals are heaped above and below them. Generally, twice as many coals should be heaped on the top as on the bottom.

Rancher's Beef Stroganoff

3 Tbsp. BUTTER	1 tsp. SALT
1 ONION, diced	1 cup WATER
1/2 lb. MUSHROOMS, sliced	2 Tbsp. TOMATO PASTE
2 lbs. ROUND STEAK	2 cups BEEF BOUILLON
2 Tbsp. FLOUR	1/2 cup SOUR CREAM
	2 cups cooked RICE

In a skillet, melt 2 tablespoons butter and sauté onion and mushrooms until onions are tender. Remove with a slotted spoon and set aside. Debone steak and remove excess fat. Cut meat into strips that are 2 1/2 inches long and 3/4 inch wide. Add remaining butter and meat strips to skillet; brown meat. In a bowl, combine flour and salt; add water and tomato paste and mix until smooth. Pour over meat. Simmer mixture over medium-low heat until meat is tender, about 1 1/4 hours. Add onion mixture and bouillon; bring to a boil. Reduce heat and stir in sour cream; heat through (do not boil). Serve over rice.

Avoiding "Beefs" with Red Meat

As there was always a supply of beef available on the trail, Cookie had to be inventive with it so that his chuck would appeal to tired cowboys' appetites. Since the wagon was usually long on beef but short on vegetables, dairy and eggs, Cookie would trade a side of beef with homesteaders when possible for whatever fresh supplies he could get.

Easy Chicken Tacos

24 TACO SHELLS
1 whole CHICKEN, cooked, deboned and shredded
1 can (7 oz.) DICED GREEN CHILES
2 ONIONS, diced
6 cups grated LONGHORN CHEESE
3 TOMATOES, diced
1/2 head LETTUCE, shredded
1 AVOCADO, sliced

Place taco shells in a preheated 300° oven for 20 minutes. In a bowl, stir together chicken, green chiles and onions. Add a portion of meat mixture to each taco; top with cheese, tomatoes, lettuce and avocado.

Sloppy Joes

1 lb. LEAN GROUND BEEF
1 ONION, diced
1 can (10.75 oz.) TOMATO SOUP
1 tsp. MUSTARD
1 Tbsp. KETCHUP
SALT and PEPPER to taste
6 HAMBURGER BUNS, buttered and toasted

In a skillet, stir beef to separate; add onion and cook until meat is brown and onion is tender. Add soup, mustard, ketchup, salt and pepper and simmer for 5-10 minutes, stirring occasionally. Serve on hamburger buns.

Cowboy Spices: *Garlic, nutmeg, ginger, cayenne, chile powder and cloves.*

Southwestern Chili Tostadas

2 lbs. GROUND BEEF
3 1/2 tsp. CHILI POWDER
2 tsp. SALT
1 tsp. SUGAR
1 lg. ONION, diced
1/2 GREEN BELL PEPPER, diced
1 can (8 oz.) TOMATO SAUCE
1 can (16 oz.) DICED TOMATOES
1 cup WATER
1 clove GARLIC, minced
1 tsp. OREGANO
1 tsp. freshly ground CUMIN SEEDS
2 Tbsp. OLIVE OIL
2 Tbsp. FLOUR
1 can (15 oz.) KIDNEY BEANS, undrained
TOSTADA SHELLS
Shredded LETTUCE
Diced TOMATOES
Grated CHEDDAR CHEESE

In a large kettle or Dutch oven, brown beef; add the next eleven ingredients. Cover and simmer for 1 hour. In a bowl, mix olive oil and flour together until smooth. Add kidney beans and mix well. Add bean mixture to meat mixture. Cover and simmer, stirring occasionally, for 30 minutes. Place tostada shells on serving plates; add a mound of chili to each and top with lettuce, tomatoes and cheese.

Pintos & Pork Chops

1 lb. PINTO BEANS	**1 clove GARLIC, minced**
6 PORK CHOPS	**1 Tbsp. CHILI POWDER**
1/4 lb. diced SALT PORK	**1 1/2 tsp. SALT**
1 ONION, diced	**1/4 tsp. PEPPER**

Place beans in a large pot; cover with water and soak overnight. Cover pot and bring beans to a boil. Reduce heat and simmer 2 hours or until beans are almost tender. In a skillet, brown pork chops, remove and set aside. Add salt pork to skillet and fry until lightly browned. Add onion and garlic and cook until onion is tender. Remove skillet from heat and stir in chili powder, salt and pepper. Add mixture to beans, mixing well. Arrange pork chops on top of beans, cover and simmer 45 minutes or until beans and chops are done.

Campfire Gravy

Chuckwagon cooks always kept a supply of browned flour on hand for a quick meal.

In a skillet, brown **FLOUR**, stirring continuously. Store in a tightly corked bottle or jar. To make gravy, combine browned flour with **PAN DRIPPINGS** or **WATER**. Season with **SALT** and **PEPPER**. Serve over biscuits or slices of bread.

Meatball & Zucchini Skillet

1 cube BEEF BOUILLON
1/2 cup BOILING WATER
2 slices BREAD, crumbled
2 tsp. chopped fresh PARSLEY
1 lb. GROUND BEEF or VEAL
1 Tbsp. OIL
1 ONION, diced
1 clove GARLIC, minced
1/2 tsp. SALT
1 tsp. grated PARMESAN CHEESE
1 can (8 oz.) TOMATO SAUCE
4 ZUCCHINI, sliced 1/4-inch thick

Dissolve bouillon in boiling water; let cool. In a bowl, combine bouillon, bread, parsley and ground beef. Shape into 16 balls; refrigerate until firm. Add oil to a skillet and sauté onion and garlic until onion is tender; remove from skillet with a slotted spoon. Add meatballs to skillet and cook until brown on all sides; drain. Add onion mixture and remaining ingredients to skillet; bring to a boil and simmer, covered, for 10 minutes or until zucchini is tender.

Green Chile Chili

2 lbs. LEAN GROUND BEEF
SALT and PEPPER to taste
2 Tbsp. OIL
2 cans (15 oz. ea.) CHILI, without beans
1 1/2 cans (16 oz. ea.) STEWED TOMATOES
1 1/2 cans (15 oz. ea.) KIDNEY BEANS, drained
1 can (11 oz.) CORN
1 GREEN CHILE, peeled, seeded and chopped
SALT to taste

Season ground beef with salt and peppr and form into 24 balls. In a skillet, heat oil; brown meatballs well, turning several times. Drain excess fat. Stir in chili, tomatoes, kidney beans and corn. Bring mixture to a boil slowly, stirring several times, and then simmer for 15 minutes. Add chile pepper and salt. Ladle into bowls. Serve with **SOURDOUGH BREAD** on the side.

The Spanish Influence

Spanish "vaqueros" were the original cowboys. They raised and herded cattle for the Spanish missions long before the first American cattle drive. Many Spanish dishes and flavors were adopted by the chuck wagon cooks. Chile peppers were an especially favored seasoning.

Chipotle   *Serrano*   *Jalapeño*   *Cuaresmeno*

Lazy P Chicken

1 cup POTATO FLAKES
1/2 cup grated PARMESAN CHEESE
1 tsp. SEASONED SALT
1 tsp. SWEET BASIL
1-2 tsp. PAPRIKA
SALT and PEPPER to taste
1 FRYER CHICKEN, skinned and cut in pieces
1/2 cup MARGARINE, melted

In a shallow bowl, combine potato flakes, cheese, seasoned salt, basil, paprika, salt and pepper; mix well. Dip chicken in margarine and then dredge in potato flake mixture. Place chicken in a baking dish; bake at 375° for 45 minutes or until tests done.

Diamond J Ham Loaf

2 lbs. ground COOKED HAM
3 EGGS, lightly beaten
1 1/2 tsp. DRY MUSTARD
1 cup SOUR CREAM
2 cups fresh BREAD CRUMBS
1/4 cup packed BROWN SUGAR

In a bowl, combine ham, eggs, 1/2 teaspoon mustard, sour cream and bread crumbs; mix well. Place in a greased loaf pan. In a small bowl, mix remaining mustard and brown sugar; spread over top of ham loaf. Bake at 350° for 1 1/4 hours.

Western Lasagna

1/2 lb. GROUND BEEF
1 ONION, diced
1 clove GARLIC, minced
1 can (16 oz.) DICED TOMATOES
1 can (12 oz.) RED CHILI SAUCE
1 can (4.25 oz.) CHOPPED BLACK OLIVES
1 tsp. SALT
1/4 tsp. PEPPER
1/4 cup OLIVE OIL

8 CORN TORTILLAS, cut in half
1/2 lb. RICOTTA CHEESE
1 EGG, beaten
1/2 lb. MONTEREY JACK CHEESE, thinly sliced
TORTILLA CHIPS
1/2 cup grated CHEDDAR CHEESE

In a large skillet, brown beef, onion and garlic; add tomatoes, chili sauce, olives, salt and pepper. Simmer 20 minutes, stirring occasionally. Set aside. In a small skillet, heat olive oil; add tortillas, one at a time, and cook until just soft. Drain on paper towels. In a bowl, mix ricotta cheese and egg. Spread 1/3 of the meat mixture in a 13 x 9 casserole dish. Top with half of the Monterey Jack cheese, then half of the ricotta cheese mixture. Add a layer of half the tortillas then a layer of meat, the remaining Monterey Jack cheese and the remaining ricotta mixture. Layer remaining tortillas and meat. Sprinkle tortilla chips and then cheddar cheese over meat. Bake at 350° for 25 minutes.

Barbequed Chicken

1/2 cup BARBEQUE SAUCE
1/2 cup KETCHUP
1 Tbsp. LEMON JUICE
1/4 cup SHERRY
1 Tbsp. WORCESTERSHIRE SAUCE
Dash of TABASCO®
2 Tbsp. BROWN SUGAR
1 (2 1/2 lb.) CHICKEN, cut in quarters

In a bowl, mix liquid ingredients together. Add brown sugar; stir until dissolved. Place chicken in a baking pan. Pour sauce over top and bake at 375° for 1 1/2 hours or until chicken is done.

Did You Know?

In the 1800's, Colonel B. H. Campbell branded his cattle with the Bar B Q sign. Somewere along the way, people started associating this brand with a certain ranch-style of cooking that became known as barbeque!

BQ

Southwestern Sloppy Joes

1/2 cup finely chopped ONION
1/4 cup fnely chopped CELERY
1 Tbsp. OIL
1 1/2 lbs. GROUND BEEF
1 can (16 oz.) TOMATO SAUCE
1/2 cup WATER
1/2 cup CHILI SAUCE
1/2 cup uncooked OATS
1 Tbsp. SALT
1 1/2 tsp. CHILI POWDER
1 tsp. WORCESTERSHIRE SAUCE
1/4 tsp. LIQUID SMOKE (optional)
4 drops TABASCO®
1/4 lb. CHEDDAR CHEESE, cubed
6-8 toasted HAMBURGER BUNS

In a skillet, sauté onion and celery in hot oil until tender but not browned. Add beef and brown. Stir in tomato sauce, water, chili sauce, oats, salt, chili powder, Worcestershire sauce, liquid smoke and Tabasco. Cover and cook over low heat until slightly thickened, about 15 minutes. Stir occasionally. Fold in cheese and serve immediately on toasted buns.

Real Cowboys

Cowboys blazed trails in more than one way. Despite Hollywood portrayals, all cowboys were not white; one out of every three cowboys was African-American, American Indian or Hispanic.

Wrangler's Pizza

1/2 cup diced ONION
1/4 cup diced CELERY
1/4 cup diced GREEN BELL PEPPER
1 Tbsp. OIL
2 lbs. LEAN GROUND BEEF, CHICKEN or TURKEY
SALT and PEPPER to taste
1 cup sliced MUSHROOMS
1 can (8 oz.) TOMATO SAUCE
1 jar (14 oz.) PIZZA SAUCE
1 cup WATER
PIZZA or BISCUIT DOUGH, for 1 pizza
Shredded MOZZARRELLA CHEESE

Preheat oven to 400°. In a large skillet, sauté onion, celery and bell pepper in oil until onion is translucent. Add ground beef, salt and pepper. Cook until meat is brown; add mushrooms, tomato sauce, pizza sauce and water. Simmer until slightly thickened. Roll pizza dough to 1/4-inch thick circle and place on a pizza pan. Spread meat mixture on dough; top with cheese. Bake for 15 minutes.

Cowboy Humor

• Horseback riding: *The art of keeping a horse between you and the ground.*

• Cowboy logic: *Never hunker down when you have your spurs on!*

Stuffed Pork Chops

Stuffing:
- 2 Tbsp. BUTTER
- 1 ONION, finely chopped
- 1/2 cup finely chopped CELERY
- 1/4 cup finely chopped NUTS
- 3/4 cup fresh BREAD CRUMBS
- 1/4 cup chopped fresh PARSLEY
- 1/4 tsp. SALT
- 1/8 tsp. freshly grated NUTMEG
- 1 EGG, lightly beaten
- Freshly ground BLACK PEPPER to taste

6 double loin PORK CHOPS with pockets
1 cup BEEF STOCK

Preheat oven to 350°. In a skillet, melt butter and sauté onion, celery and nuts until onion is soft. Remove from heat. Add remaining stuffing ingredients to onion mixture; mix well. Spoon stuffing into pork chop pockets. Place chops in a shallow baking dish, cover with foil and bake for 1 hour, turning chops after 30 minutes. Uncover and continue baking for 30 minutes or until well browned. Remove chops to a platter and keep warm. Drain excess fat from the baking pan, add beef stock and heat, scraping loose any browned particles remaining in the pan. Cook sauce until heated through and pour over the pork chops.

Lazy Bar H Pecan Chicken

2 Tbsp. OIL
1 ONION, sliced
8 CHICKEN BREASTS, halved and boned
1/4 cup diced PRUNES
1/4 cup RUM
1/4 cup MOLASSES
1/4 tsp. ALLSPICE
1/4 cup coarsely chopped PECANS

In a large skillet, heat oil and sauté onion until translucent. Remove onion from skillet and set aside. Add chicken to skillet and cook until lightly browned on all sides. In a bowl, combine sautéed onion, prunes, rum, molasses and allspice; pour mixture over chicken. Cover skillet and cook on low heat for 40 minutes, turning chicken once. Remove cover and stir in pecans. Cook for 10 minutes or until chicken is tender and juices run clear.

Cowboy Lingo

Food: *Chuck, grub, chow*
Beans: *Pecos strawberries, frijoles*
Biscuits: *Sourdough bullets*
Meringue: *Calf slobbers*
Woman: *A calico*
Stetson Hat: *John B.*
Fiddling: *Agitating the cat guts*

WORLD'S GREATEST TRICK ROPE COWBOY

Big Beef Casserole

2 lbs. GROUND BEEF	1/3 cup chopped
1 ONION, diced	PARSLEY
1/2 cup BUTTER	1/2 tsp. PEPPER
8 oz. MACARONI,	1/2 tsp. CINNAMON
cooked and drained	3 tsp. SALT
1/2 cup KETCHUP	1/3 cup FLOUR
1/2 cup WATER	2 1/2 cups MILK
1 cup grated CHEDDAR	1 tsp. DRY MUSTARD
CHEESE	3 EGGS, lightly beaten

In a skillet, sauté ground beef and onions in 2 tablespoons butter until brown. Add macaroni, ketchup, water, 1/2 cup cheese, parsley, pepper, cinnamon and 2 teaspoons salt; mix thoroughly. Place meat mixture in a greased 13 x 9 baking pan. In a saucepan, melt the remaining butter; stir in flour and cook until bubbly. Gradually stir in milk. Add mustard and remaining salt and cook until thick. Whisk in eggs, in small portions. When well mixed, pour over meat mixture. Top with remaining cheese. Bake at 350° for 30 minutes.

Dutch Oven Magic

Cookie used his Dutch oven to prepare most any kind of meal. From stews and tough cuts of beef to biscuits, cobblers and pies, trail cooks proved that almost anything can be cooked with just a Dutch oven and a hot fire.

Chuck Wagon Pie

1 ONION, diced
1 Tbsp. OIL
1 lb. GROUND BEEF
SALT and PEPPER to taste
1 can (14 oz.) GREEN BEANS, drained
1 can (10.75 oz.) TOMATO SOUP
5 POTATOES, cooked and mashed
1/2 cup WARM MILK
1 EGG, beaten

In a large skillet, sauté onion in oil until translucent. Add ground beef, salt and pepper. Cook until meat is browned. Add beans and soup; stir. Pour mixture into a greased 1 1/2-quart casserole dish. In a separate bowl, combine mashed potatoes, milk and egg. Mix well; spread mixture over top of meat. Bake for 30 minutes at 350°.

Corned Beef Hash

3 Tbsp. OIL
4 POTATOES, peeled and sliced
1 ONION, sliced
1 GREEN CHILE, peeled, seeded and chopped
1 can (12 oz.) CORNED BEEF

In a skillet, heat oil; add potatoes and fry until half done. Add onion and chili. Add corned beef to skillet. Stir and cook until potatoes are done.

Bean & Biscuit Casserole

1/2 cup chopped ONION
3/4 cup chopped GREEN BELL PEPPER
2 Tbsp. BUTTER or MARGARINE
1 lb. HOT DOGS, sliced
1 can (16 oz.) PORK AND BEANS
1/3 cup CHILI SAUCE
1/3 cup KETCHUP
1-2 Tbsp. BROWN SUGAR (optional)
2 cans (10 oz. ea.) BUTTERMILK BISCUITS
3/4 cup grated CHEDDAR CHEESE
1/2 cup crushed CORN CHIPS
3 Tbsp. grated ROMANO or PARMESAN CHEESE
Addititional BUTTER

In large skillet, sauté onion and bell pepper in 1 tablespoon butter. Stir in hot dogs, pork and beans, chili sauce, ketchup and brown sugar; simmer for 2 minutes. Separate biscuit dough into 10 biscuits; pull each apart into halves. Arrange 10 biscuit pieces in bottom of an ungreased 12 x 8 pan. Spoon meat mixture over biscuits. Sprinkle with cheddar cheese. Top with remaining biscuit halves. In a bowl, combine corn chips and Romano cheese; sprinkle over biscuits. Dot with butter. Bake at 375° for 20 minutes until biscuits are golden brown.

The Nutritious Bean

Although the cowboys didn't know it, beans provided much-needed nutrients: protein, calcium, phosphorous, fiber and vitamins.

Grilled Chicken & Prickly Pear Salsa

Prickly Pear Salsa:
- 1/2 lg. CANTALOUPE
- 1/2 lg. HONEYDEW MELON
- 1 lg. PINEAPPLE
- 1 RED PEPPER, finely diced
- 1 RED ONION, finely diced
- 1 bunch GREEN ONIONS, finely diced
- 1 bunch CILANTRO, finely chopped
- JUICE of 1 LEMON
- 1 Tbsp. CUMIN
- 1 cup PRICKLY PEAR SYRUP

4 CHICKEN BREASTS

To make salsa, cut cantaloupe, honeydew and pineapple into 1/4-inch pieces. Place fruit and vegetables in a bowl. Squeeze lemon juice over the mixture; add cumin. Pour prickly pear syrup over all and stir. Grill chicken breasts. When done, pile salsa on chicken and serve immediately.

Good Old Boy's Meat Loaf

3/4 cup MILK
1 1/2 cups BREAD CRUMBS
2 lbs. GROUND BEEF
2 tsp. SALT
1/4 tsp. PEPPER
1 CARROT, grated

1 ONION, diced
2 EGGS, beaten
1/4 cup KETCHUP
3 Tbsp. BROWN
　　SUGAR
2 Tbsp. MUSTARD

In a bowl, combine milk and bread crumbs and toss until crumbs are moistened. Add ground beef, salt, pepper, carrot, onion and eggs. Mix thoroughly. Place mixture in a 9 x 5 loaf pan. In a small bowl, mix ketchup, brown sugar and mustard; spread over meat loaf. Bake at 325° for 1 1/2 hours.

Lazy Q's Pot Roast

4-5 lb. BOTTOM ROUND ROAST
1 can (10.75 oz.) CREAM OF MUSHROOM SOUP
1 pkg. (2.5 oz.) ONION SOUP MIX

Preheat oven to 375°. Place meat in a roasting pan. Spread cream of mushroom soup over meat; sprinkle with soup mix. Cover pan tightly with heavy duty aluminum foil and bake, allowing 45 minutes cooking time per pound.

Mini Meat Loaves

1 1/2 lbs. GROUND BEEF
1 ONION, chopped
1 EGG
1/4 cup DRY BREAD CRUMBS
1/4 cup chopped GREEN BELL PEPPER
1/2 cup WATER
1/4 cup LEMON JUICE
1 tsp. SALT
1/2 tsp. dry instant BEEF BOUILLON
6 thin slices BACON, cut into halves, crosswise

Preheat oven to 350°. In a bowl, mix together all ingredients except bacon. Shape mixture into six mini-loaves and place them in a shallow baking pan. Criss-cross 2 half-slices bacon on each loaf, tucking under ends. Bake, uncovered, for 50 minutes.

Cowboy Talk

Whiskey: *Bottled Courage, Tornado Juice, Fire-water, Redeye, Joy Juice, Snake Pizen*

Chuck Wagon Cook: *Pot Russler, Cookie, Sourdough, Greasy Belly, Dough Puncher*

Cowboy: *Cowhand, Trail Hand, Driver, Cow Poke, Buckaroo, Ranger, Rider, Waddy, Cow Puncher*

Grilled Leg of Lamb

2 legs (5-6 lbs. ea.) LAMB, boned and butterflied
6-8 cloves GARLIC, slivered

Marinade:

1/2 cup LEMON JUICE	**1 Tbsp. OREGANO**
1/2 cup OLIVE OIL	**2 tsp. HICKORY**
1 tsp. PEPPER	**SMOKED SALT**

In a large shallow dish, lay lamb legs out flat. Make tiny slits on both sides of meat and insert slivers of garlic. In a bowl, mix together marinade ingredients; pour evenly over lamb. Turn meat to coat other side; cover and refrigerate at least 12 hours. Grill over medium coals. For medium rare, allow 20 minutes per side. Slice and serve.

Sausage Casserole

1 lb. BULK PORK SAUSAGE
4 stalks CELERY, diced
1 GREEN BELL PEPPER, diced
1 ONION, diced
3 pkgs. (4.5 oz. ea.) CHICKEN NOODLE SOUP
2 cups uncooked LONG GRAIN RICE
1 cup chopped ALMONDS

Simmer sausage, celery, bell pepper and onion until sausage is lightly browned and vegetables are tender but not brown. Prepare soup according to package directions. Combine sausage mixture and soup in a large casserole dish. Add rice and almonds and mix well. Bake at 350° for 1 hour.

Oven-Dried Beef Jerky

Cowboys often carried a supply of jerky to eat during the long nights of cattle tending.

2-2 1/2 lbs. boneless BEEF

Marinade:

1 cup WATER	1/4 tsp. BLACK PEPPER
2 Tbsp. LIQUID SMOKE	1 tsp. GARLIC SALT
1/4 tsp. SALT	1 tsp. LEMON PEPPER

Trim fat from meat and cut into strips that are 6 inches long and 1/8-inch thick. Place strips in a glass casserole dish. In a bowl, combine marinade ingredients and stir well. Pour over beef. Cover and marinate overnight in refrigerator, stirring occasionally. Drain and dry meat thoroughly. Cover bottom rack of oven with aluminum foil. Arrange strips of meat close together on oven rack; do not overlap. Bake at 150°-175° for 10-12 hours. Beef is done when pieces feel dry, not crisp. Store in airtight containers.

Home Cooking on the Range

The way the trail cook prepared food depended on where he was from and who had influenced his style of cooking. Most often, his influences were southern, Texan and Mexican. But every once in a while, there was a Yankee touch to some recipe—most likely because it came from a New England homesteader.

Beef & Bean Casserole

1 1/2 lbs. GROUND BEEF
2 cans (15 oz. ea.) KIDNEY BEANS
2 cans (11 oz. ea.) PORK AND BEANS
1 ONION, diced
1 GREEN BELL PEPPER, diced
3 Tbsp. BROWN SUGAR
1 can (4 oz.) DICED GREEN CHILES
TABASCO to taste
1 cup TOMATO or BARBECUE SAUCE

In a skillet, cook beef until brown; drain. In a bowl, combine remaining ingredients; stir in meat. Ladle mixture into a 13 x 9 casserole dish and bake at 350° for 30-45 minutes.

Stuffed Spareribs

3 Tbsp. OIL
1 ONION, finely chopped
3 cups cubed BREAD
1 1/2 cups crushed POTATO CHIPS
1 cup BOUILLON
1 cup finely chopped APPLE
1/2 cup finely chopped CELERY
1 tsp. SALT
1/4 tsp. PEPPER

In a skillet, heat oil and sauté onion until translucent. Remove skillet from heat and stir in remaining ingredients. Cut **4 lbs. SPARERIBS** into two sections of equal length; sprinkle with **SALT** and **PEPPER**. Place one section in a baking pan, layer with stuffing; top with second section. Secure with skewers and bake at 350° for 2 hours.

Cookie's Favorite Pot Roast

5 lb. VENISON or BEEF ROAST (any cut)
2 Tbsp. VEGETABLE OIL
5 POTATOES, cubed
2 ONIONS, coarsely chopped
4 CARROTS, diagonally sliced
3/4 cup sliced CELERY
2 GREEN BELL PEPPERS, coarsely chopped

Sauce:
   2 cups KETCHUP
   1/2 cup BURGUNDY WINE or TOMATO JUICE
   3 Tbsp. BALSAMIC VINEGAR
   3 Tbsp. WORCESTERSHIRE SAUCE
   2 Tbsp. fresh LEMON JUICE
   2 Tbsp. BROWN SUGAR
   3/4 cup WATER
   2 Tbsp. CHILI POWDER
   2 Tbsp. PARSLEY
   2 Tbsp. MUSTARD
   1 Tbsp. CORNSTARCH
   1/4 cup COLD WATER

   In a large skillet, brown meat in oil; place in a roasting pan and surround with vegetables. Mix together all sauce ingredients except cornstarch and water. Pour over meat and vegetables. Bake at 275° for 4 hours. Remove meat and vegetables to a serving platter and pour desired amount of sauce for gravy into a saucepan. Heat, adding cornstarch mixed with cold water to thicken.

Shorty's Short Ribs

4-4 1/2 lbs. BEEF SHORT RIBS
1 Tbsp. OLIVE OIL
2 cups APPLE JUICE or WATER
1/4 cup finely chopped ONION
1 tsp. SALT
1/2 tsp. coarsely ground PEPPER
1/2 tsp. WHOLE ALLSPICE
2 BAY LEAVES
1 Tbsp. FLOUR
1/4 cup WATER
1 cup SOUR CREAM

In a Dutch oven or large kettle, over medium-high heat, brown short ribs in oil on all sides. In a bowl, stir together apple juice, onion, salt, pepper, allspice and bay leaves; pour over meat. Cover and cook over low heat about 2 hours or until meat is tender. Remove meat to a serving plate; keep warm. For gravy, combine flour and water; stir into pan liquids. Cook, stirring constantly, until thickened. Blend in sour cream; heat through. Strain and serve on the side.

Serves 4.

White Gold?

Salt was sometimes referred to as "white gold" because of its value to the chuck wagon cook who used it not only for seasoning but for preserving meat and other foods. At times, salt could cost four times more than the meat itself!

South-of-the-Border Beef Tacos

1 lb. LEAN GROUND BEEF
1 Tbsp. OLIVE OIL
3/4 cup chopped ONION
1 clove GARLIC, minced
1 tsp. SALT
2 cans (4 oz. ea.) GREEN CHILES, finely chopped
2 cans (4.25 oz. ea.) chopped RIPE OLIVES
1 can (8 oz.) TOMATO SAUCE
OIL for frying
8 CORN TORTILLAS
Shredded LETTUCE
Grated MONTEREY JACK CHEESE
Sliced AVOCADO

In a skillet, brown beef in olive oil, adding onion and garlic when meat is halfway done. Add salt, chiles, olives and tomato sauce. Cook over low heat for 5 minutes. Fry tortillas lightly in oil. Fold in half, holding with fork to shape. Drain well on paper towels. Fill tortillas with meat mixture. Top with lettuce, cheese and avocado as desired.

Chile con Carne

2 lbs. dried PINTO BEANS
2 Tbsp. SALT
2 lbs. chopped BEEF
2 ONIONS, diced
4 cloves GARLIC, minced
1 can (4 oz.) DICED GREEN CHILES
1 can (12 oz.) TACO SAUCE
1 can (16 oz.) DICED TOMATOES
1/2 tsp. BLACK PEPPER
1/2 tsp. CUMIN SEED

Soak pinto beans in cold water overnight; drain and wash. In a Dutch oven or large kettle, cover beans with 2 inches of water; add salt and simmer over moderate heat for 1 hour, adding water if needed. In a skillet, brown beef and then add with remaining ingredients to the beans. Cook, covered, over reduced heat for 1-1 1/2 hours or until beans are tender.

The First Assembly Line?

In 1869, James First joined with Rosenfield and Charles Benser to form the Moline Wagon Company. This company produced more than one million wagons by 1909! Employing more than 500 workers, the company claimed it could build a new wagon every 30 minutes!

Side Dishes

Canned Delights!

Most of the cowboy's fruits and vegetables were only available in cans. The cowboys called canned goods "airtights." Although fruits were a welcome addition to their fare, vegetables were considered "unmanly" and were rarely included.

Most milk came from a can, too.

Eggs were definitely a luxury. When the cowboy was in town, his favorite order of the day was ham and "States' eggs" (eggs imported from the eastern states).

Southwestern Barbeque Sauce

2 Tbsp. OIL
1/4 cup finely chopped ONIONS
1/4 cup finely chopped CELERY
1/2 Tbsp. PAPRIKA
1 tsp. SALT
Juice of 1/2 LEMON
1/4 cup packed BROWN SUGAR
1/4 cup VINEGAR
1 GREEN BELL PEPPER, chopped
1 jar (12 oz.) CHILI SAUCE
1 Tbsp. WORCESTERSHIRE SAUCE
3 drops TABASCO®
1/4 cup WATER
1 Tbsp. MUSTARD

In a skillet, heat oil; sauté onions and celery until tender. Add remaining ingredients in the order listed, stirring after each addition. Simmer for 30 minutes. Refrigerate in a covered glass or ceramic dish.

Makes 1 quart.

Green Chile Rice

1 tsp. SALT
1 cup SOUR CREAM
1/2 cup grated CHEDDAR CHEESE
1/2 cup grated MONTEREY JACK CHEESE
3 1/2 cups cooked RICE
1 can (4 oz.) GREEN CHILES, drained and chopped
1 can (4 oz.) PIMENTOS, drained and chopped

Preheat oven to 350°. In a bowl, combine salt and sour cream. Add both cheeses and stir until blended. Add cooked rice, chiles and pimentos and mix well. Spread mixture in a greased 9 x 9 baking pan and bake for 45 minutes. Serve hot.

Sweet Pinto Beans

2 lbs. dried PINTO BEANS   **1 clove GARLIC, minced**
1 tsp. SALT   **1 cup diced ONION**
1 tsp. CHILI POWDER   **6 slices BACON, chopped**
1/4 cup packed BROWN   **1 cup BARBECUE**
SUGAR   **SAUCE**

Wash beans and place in a 2-quart crockpot. Cover with water and bring to a boil. Boil for 30 minutes; drain, rinse and return to crockpot. Add remaining ingredients and water to cover. Cook on high heat 6-8 hours or on low heat for 10-12 hours, adding water as needed to keep beans covered.

Baked Corn Pudding

2 cups FRESH CORN,
   cut from cob
2 EGGS, beaten
1 cup MILK

1 Tbsp. SUGAR
1 tsp. SALT
1/8 tsp. PEPPER

Place corn in a greased baking dish. In a bowl, combine eggs, milk, sugar, salt and pepper. Whisk until well blended. Pour mixture over corn. Place baking dish in a pan of boiling water and bake at 400° for 40 minutes.

Scalloped Potatoes

4 med. POTATOES, thinly sliced
1/4 tsp. ONION SALT
1/4 tsp. BLACK PEPPER
MILK, as needed
1/4 cup grated CHEDDAR CHEESE
Sprig of PARSLEY, chopped

Place half the potato slices in greased casserole dish. Season with 1/8 teaspoon onion salt and 1/8 teaspoon pepper. Layer remaining potatoes and season with remaining onion salt and pepper. Add milk until potatoes are covered. Top with cheddar cheese. Bake at 300° for 45 minutes. Garnish with parsley.

Cornmeal Pie

1 cup BUTTER or MARGARINE
1 cup SUGAR
4 EGGS, beaten
1 can (4 oz.) DICED GREEN CHILES
1 can (15 oz.) CREAM STYLE CORN
1/2 cup shredded CHEDDAR CHEESE
1/2 cup shredded MONTEREY JACK CHEESE
1 cup FLOUR
1 cup YELLOW CORNMEAL
4 tsp. BAKING POWDER
Pinch of SALT

In a bowl, cream together butter and sugar. Add eggs gradually to creamed mixture, beating well after each addition. Stir in green chiles, corn and cheese. In a separate bowl, sift together flour, cornmeal, baking powder and salt. Combine mixtures and pour into a greased and floured 12 x 8 baking dish. Bake at 300° for 1 hour.

Refried Beans

2 Tbsp. OIL
1 sm. ONION, finely chopped
3 cups cooked PINTO BEANS, broth reserved
1 1/2 cups reserved BEAN BROTH

Heat oil in a large skillet, add onion and sauté until translucent. Add beans, a small amount at a time, mashing them with a large fork; add some of the broth after each addition. Heat thoroughly.

Piñon Nut Potato Casserole

6 med. POTATOES, unpeeled and diced
1/4 cup shelled PIÑON NUTS
1 cup SMALL CURD COTTAGE CHEESE
1/2 cup SOUR CREAM
1/4 cup minced ONION
SALT and PEPPER to taste
TOASTED ALMONDS
BUTTER or MARGARINE, as needed

In a large pot, cover potatoes with water and bring to a boil; simmer until potatoes are tender. Place the pine nuts in a small skillet and toast over medium-high heat, stirring constantly with a wooden spoon. Drain potatoes well and add piñon nuts. Add cottage cheese, sour cream, onion, salt and pepper to potato mixture. Beat with an electric mixer until creamy. (Adjust the proportions of cottage cheese and sour cream to suit taste and texture.) Spoon mixture into a lightly buttered casserole dish. Sprinkle toasted almonds on top. Dot with butter. Bake, uncovered, at 350° for 30 minutes.

Piñon Nuts

Piñon nuts come from pine trees. They are found in the pine cones of several varieties of pine trees in the Southwestern states.

Salsa

Many variations of salsas were developed by the cowboy cooks. Hotter chiles, garlic, chili powder, and vinegar were added to suit each cook's tastes.

2 cups peeled TOMATOES, chopped
1 stalk CELERY, diced
1 ONION, diced
1 GREEN BELL PEPPER, diced
1 tsp. SALT
1 Tbsp. VINEGAR
1 Tbsp. SUGAR
1 GREEN CHILE, peeled, seeded and chopped

In a bowl, combine all ingredients and blend well. Cover tightly and chill overnight.

Skillet Mac & Cheese

1/4 cup BUTTER
1 cup chopped ONION
1 Tbsp. FLOUR
1 tsp. SALT
1/4 tsp. OREGANO

1 pkg. (8 oz.) ELBOW
  MACARONI
3 1/2 cups MILK
2 cups shredded
  CHEDDAR CHEESE

In a skillet, melt butter. Add onion and sauté until tender. Stir in flour, salt, oregano, macaroni and milk. Cover and bring to a boil. Reduce heat and simmer, stirring occasionally, for 15 minutes or until macaroni is tender. Add cheese and stir until cheese is melted.

Barbequed Beans

1 lb. CANADIAN BACON	2 tsp. liquid GRAVY MIX
1/2 cup diced ONION	1/4 tsp. MARJORAM
1 clove GARLIC, minced	1/4 tsp. SALT
2 cans (16 oz. ea.) PORK	1 tsp. DRY MUSTARD
and BEANS	1/2 cup MOLASSES

Cut bacon into 1/4-inch thick slices and then cut into large squares. Place in a large skillet and cook until brown and slightly crisp. Add onion and garlic and cook until onions are just tender, about 5 minutes. Add pork and beans, gravy mix, marjoram, salt and mustard. Drizzle molasses over top; mix lightly but well. Cover and cook over low heat for 30 minutes. Remove cover and continue cooking for 15 minutes, stirring occasionally.

Prairie Lima Beans

6 slices BACON, cut in small pieces
1 ONION, chopped
1/2 tsp. SALT
1 clove GARLIC, crushed
1/4 cup chopped GREEN BELL PEPPER
1 can (8 oz.) TOMATO SAUCE
2 cans (16 oz. ea.) LIMA BEANS, drained
Grated PARMESAN CHEESE

In a saucepan, cook bacon until crisp. Drain, reserving 3 tablespoons of drippings. Add onion, salt, garlic and bell pepper. Sauté until vegetables are tender. Add tomato sauce and lima beans. Simmer 15 minutes at medium heat. Ladle into serving dish and garnish with Parmesan cheese.

Flour Tortillas

2 cups FLOUR
1 tsp. SALT
1 1/2 tsp. BAKING POWDER

1 Tbsp. SHORTENING
COLD WATER

In a bowl, combine first four ingredients. Add enough cold water to make a stiff dough. Knead dough until smooth and elastic; roll into small balls and then pat out very thin. Heat 30 seconds in a hot skillet; flip and cook another 30 seconds.

Tortillas: Bred On The Range

Tortilla: a name given by the Spaniards to the unleavened flat bread they found among the Aztec in the sixteenth century. The word <u>tortilla</u> comes from the Spanish word <u>torta</u> which means "round cake." Use of the tortilla spread northward, eventually finding its way to the cowboy campfire.

Corn Tortillas

2 cups CORNMEAL or MASA HARINA
1 tsp. SALT
WARM WATER

In a bowl, combine cornmeal, salt and enough water to make a stiff dough. Let sit for 15-20 minutes. Roll dough into balls about the size of an egg and then pat into thin rounds. In a skillet, cook over medium-high heat for 30 seconds, flip and cook another 30 seconds.

Glazed Carrots

12 BABY CARROTS, peeled
2 Tbsp. BUTTER
1/3 cup HONEY
1 Tbsp. LEMON JUICE
1/2 cup canned CRUSHED PINEAPPLE, drained

In a saucepan, bring a small amount of salted water to a boil. Add whole carrots and cook, covered, until slightly tender. Melt butter in a skillet; add honey, lemon juice and pineapple. Add carrots to skillet and turn to coat evenly. Cook over low heat until well glazed.

Skillet Tomatoes

1/4 cup BUTTER
1/2 cup finely chopped ONION
2 Tbsp. chopped PARSLEY
1/2 tsp. SALT
1/4 tsp. THYME
1/8 tsp. PEPPER
6 whole TOMATOES, peeled and cored

Melt butter in a skillet. Add onion, parsley, salt, thyme and pepper and stir. Place tomatoes on top of onion mixture and cover. Cook 5 minutes. Turn tomatoes and baste with seasonings. Cover and cook an additional 5 minutes.

Breads, Biscuits & Muffins

Sourdough Starter

(A Modern Version)

2 cups WARM WATER   **2 cups FLOUR**
1 pkg. active DRY YEAST   **1/4 tsp. SUGAR**

Place 1/2 cup of warm water in a glass or ceramic bowl; add yeast and let dissolve. Add flour, sugar and remaining water to mixture. Mix well; cover with a towel and set in a warm place for at least 48 hours. Refrigerate, loosely covered.

To keep starter active: every two weeks, remove at least 1 cup of starter and replenish by adding equal quantities of warm water and flour. Let mixture stand at room temperature for 8 hours before loosely covering and returning to refrigerator.

Sourdough Starters

Sourdough starters act as a leavening and flavoring agent for breads, pancakes and biscuits. Sourdough was a staple for many ranch and chuck wagon cooks.

Cowboy-Style Starter

Cowboy cooks relied on the fermentation of an acid, such as vinegar or grape juice, for their sourdough starters. Here's an authentic cowboy starter.

Put **2 cups FLOUR** in a crock or pail with a lid. Add **2 tablespoons SUGAR** and **1 tablespoon SALT**. Mix well. Stir in **1 1/2 cups WATER** and beat to a smooth dough. Add **1 tablespoon VINEGAR** to the batter and set in a warm place to ferment. After using starter, replenish with **1 cup FLOUR** and **1 cup WATER**.

Sourdough Cornbread

1 cup SOURDOUGH STARTER (see pg. 69)
1 1/2 cups YELLOW CORNMEAL
1 1/2 cups EVAPORATED MILK
2 EGGS, beaten
2 Tbsp. SUGAR
1/4 cup BUTTER, melted
1/2 tsp. SALT
3/4 tsp. BAKING SODA

In a large bowl, thoroughly mix sourdough starter, cornmeal, milk, eggs and sugar. Stir in butter, salt and baking soda. Pour into an 8-inch loaf pan and bake at 450° for 30 minutes. Cool on rack before removing from pan.

Sourdough Muffins

1/2 cup SOURDOUGH STARTER (see pg. 69)
1 cup MILK
2 1/2 cups FLOUR
1 Tbsp. SUGAR
1 tsp. SALT
1/2 tsp. BAKING SODA
CORNMEAL, as needed

In a large mixing bowl, combine sourdough starter, milk and 2 cups of flour. Mix together; cover and let sit at room temperature about 8 hours. In a separate bowl, mix remaining flour, sugar, salt and baking soda. Sprinkle mixture over the dough and mix thoroughly. Place dough on a lightly floured board and knead for 2-3 minutes. Roll dough out to 3/4-inch thickness. Cut out muffins with a 3-inch cookie cutter. Place muffins 1-inch apart on cookie sheets; cover with a towel and let rise for 1 hour. Sprinkle both sides of muffins with cornmeal; bake in a 300° oven for 10 minutes. Turn muffins over and bake another 10 minutes.

Stick Bread

When a cowboy had no stove, not even a Dutch oven in which to bake his bread, he simply rolled his dough (flour and water) around the end of a stick and placed it over the campfire coals to bake.

Cookie's Sourdough Biscuits

Biscuits were a staple in a cowboy's life, and a Cookie was judged by his biscuits.

1 1/2 cups ALL-PURPOSE FLOUR
2 tsp. BAKING POWDER
1/4 tsp. BAKING SODA
1/2 tsp. SALT
1/4 cup BUTTER, melted
1 cup SOURDOUGH STARTER (see pg. 69)

Sift dry ingredients together. Blend in butter and sourdough starter and mix well. Roll dough out onto a floured surface until 1/2-inch thick. Cut into 12 rounds or squares and place on greased baking sheets. Cover and let rise 30 minutes. Bake at 450° for 20 minutes or until golden brown.

Edible Cactus!?

Cowboys found, through trial and error, and recipe swapping with Native Peoples, that certain types of cactus can be turned into food items, fit for human consumption. For instance, prickly pear cactus fruits are used in making cactus jelly and cactus candy; the "pads" (often referred to as "nopales"), when prepared properly, can be eaten raw, pickled or cooked. The fruit of the majestic saguaro can also be made into a jam or jelly.

Sourdough Bread

1 cup SOURDOUGH
   STARTER (see pg. 69)
1 qt. LUKEWARM WATER
3/4 cup SUGAR

2 Tbsp. SALT
1 cup OIL
1 1/2 cups FLOUR

In a bowl, combine sourdough starter and remaining ingredients. Place dough on a lightly-floured board and knead until smooth and pliable; put in a greased bowl and let rise until doubled. Punch down and knead; let rise again until doubled. Divide dough into four loaves; place them in greased 9 x 5 loaf pans. Allow dough to double again in size. Bake at 400° for 35-40 minutes.

Spoon Bread

This cornbread is so rich and dense, it must be served up with a spoon!

3 cups MILK
1 1/4 cups WHITE
   CORNMEAL
3 EGGS, beaten

2 Tbsp. BUTTER, melted
1 3/4 tsp. BAKING
   POWDER
1 tsp. SALT

In a double boiler, bring milk to a rapid boil. Slowly add cornmeal, stirring constantly until thick. Remove from heat and allow to cool. Add eggs, butter, baking powder and salt. Beat with electric mixer at medium speed for 5 minutes. Pour batter into a greased 12 x 8 casserole and bake at 375° for 30 minutes. Serve by spoonfuls from casserole.

Olive Nut Bread

1 1/2 cups BUTTERMILK
1 EGG, lightly beaten
3 cups BISCUIT MIX
2 Tbsp. SUGAR
1 cup grated SWISS CHEESE
1 cup drained and sliced PIMENTO-STUFFED
    OLIVES
3/4 cup chopped WALNUTS

In a bowl, combine buttermilk, egg, biscuit mix and sugar; beat for 1 minute to blend thoroughly. Gently stir in cheese, olives and walnuts. Spoon batter into a well-buttered 9 x 5 loaf pan. Bake at 350° for 50-55 minutes. Remove from oven and cool 5 minutes before removing from pan. Continue cooling on wire rack before slicing.

Corn Fritters

1/2 cup FLOUR
1/2 tsp. BAKING POWDER
1/2 tsp. SALT
1/4 tsp. PAPRIKA

1 cup CORN
1 EGG, separated
OIL for frying

In a bowl, combine dry ingredients. Add corn to mixture and stir well. In a separate bowl, beat egg yolk lightly; stir thoroughly into batter. In another bowl, beat egg white until stiff; fold into batter. Carefully drop tablespoons of batter into hot oil and fry until golden brown. Serve with syrup on the side.

Whole-Wheat Bread

2 cups WHOLE-WHEAT FLOUR
1 cup WHITE FLOUR
3 tsp. BAKING POWDER
1/2 tsp. SALT
2 Tbsp. SUGAR
1/2 cup chopped NUTS
1 1/2 cups MILK
3 Tbsp. OIL

Preheat oven to 350°. Combine dry ingredients, including nuts. Add milk and blend thoroughly. Add oil; beat well. Pour batter into a well-greased shallow loaf pan or muffin pans. Bake for 30 minutes.

Lazy Z Pecan Rolls

12 tsp. BUTTER
12 tsp. BROWN SUGAR
Chopped PECANS
1 pkg. (12 ct.) BROWN and SERVE ROLLS

Preheat oven to 375°. Place 1 teaspoon butter and 1 teaspoon brown sugar in each cup of a greased 12-cup muffin pan. Place pan in oven and heat until butter has melted; remove and stir each cup to dissolve sugar. Sprinkle a few chopped pecans into each cup. Add rolls and bake for 15-20 minutes. Remove from oven and invert pan (sugar mixture will flow down over sides of rolls).

Cowboy Cornbread

1 can (15 oz.) CREAM STYLE CORN
1 cup YELLOW CORNMEAL
1 EGG, lightly beaten
1/2 tsp. BAKING SODA
1/3 cup BUTTER, melted
1 cup CONDENSED MILK
1/2 cup grated CHEDDAR CHEESE
1 can (4 oz.) DICED GREEN CHILES

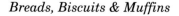

In a bowl, combine corn, cornmeal, egg, baking soda, butter and milk; stir well. Spread half of the batter in a greased 13 x 9 baking pan. Sprinkle half of the cheese over the top. Pour remaining batter over cheese. Layer chiles on top of batter; sprinkle with remaining cheese. Bake at 350° for 40 minutes or until toothpick inserted in center comes out clean.

Dutch Ovens

A Dutch oven is a three-legged iron kettle with a heavy iron lid that has turned up edges. The oven, used by chuck wagon cooks for many purposes including their sourdough or "risin' bread" was placed directly on hot coals with more coals piled on the lid. The same ovens are used today by many outdoor cooks, while more modern, flat bottom ovens are used over stoves and outdoor grills.

Oatmeal Bread

2 cups BOILING WATER
1 cup crushed OATS
1 Tbsp. OIL
1/2 cup packed BROWN SUGAR
1 tsp. SALT
4 1/2 cups FLOUR
2/3 cake COMPRESSED YEAST
1/2 cup LUKEWARM WATER

In a bowl, pour boiling water over oats. Stir in oil and let set for 2 hours. Add brown sugar, salt and flour to mixture. Dissolve yeast in lukewarm water and add to oat mixture. Beat well and let stand until doubled in size. Stir dough and then shape into 2 loaves. Place in greased loaf pans; let rise until doubled in size (about 2 hours). Bake at 375° for 1 hour or until a toothpick inserted near the center comes out clean.

Hoecakes

"Hoecakes" came from a Southern tradition of cooking cornbread on a hot hoe!

1 Tbsp. BACON   1 cup CORNMEAL
   DRIPPINGS   1 cup BOILING WATER
1 tsp. SALT

In a bowl, combine all ingredients. Stir, then let set; cornmeal will swell. Pour 1/4-1/2 cup batter into a hot, well-oiled frying pan. When bottom is brown, turn and brown the other side.

Strawberry Bread

3 cups FLOUR
1 tsp. BAKING SODA
1 tsp. SALT
3 tsp. CINNAMON
2 cups SUGAR
3 EGGS, beaten
2 pkgs. (10 oz. ea.) FROZEN
     STRAWBERRIES, thawed
1/4 cup OIL or WATER
1 1/4 cups chopped PECANS

In a large bowl, mix together flour, baking soda, salt, cinnamon and sugar. Make a well in the center and add remaining ingredients. Stir mixture thoroughly. Pour into 2 greased and floured 8-inch loaf pans. Bake at 350° for 1 hour or until a toothpick inserted near the center comes out clean.

Buttermilk Biscuits

2 cups FLOUR
1 Tbsp. SUGAR
1 Tbsp. BAKING POWDER
3/4 tsp. SALT
1/2 tsp. BAKING SODA
1/3 cup BUTTER
1 cup BUTTERMILK

Sift dry ingredients together. Cut in butter until mixture is crumbly. Add buttermilk and mix until well blended. Turn onto a floured board and knead lightly. Roll out dough to 1/2 inch thick and cut out biscuits. Arrange on a greased baking pan and bake at 450° for 15 minutes or until golden.

Banana Chocolate Chip Muffins

2 cups FLOUR
1 1/2 tsp. BAKING POWDER
1/4 tsp. BAKING SODA
1/4 tsp. SALT
1/2 cup BUTTER, softened
1/2 cup packed BROWN SUGAR
2 lg. EGGS, beaten
2 lg. BANANAS, mashed
1/3 cup MILK
1 tsp. VANILLA
3/4 cup coarsely chopped WALNUTS
3/4 cup SEMISWEET CHOCOLATE CHIPS

In a bowl, combine flour, baking powder, baking soda and salt. In a separate bowl, cream butter and brown sugar until light. Beat eggs into creamed mixture; stir in banana, milk and vanilla. Add dry ingredients and stir gently. Stir walnuts and chocolate chips into the batter, reserving 2 tablespoons of each. Spoon batter into a lightly-greased 12-cup muffin tin. Sprinkle tops with reserved walnuts and chocolate chips. Bake at 375° for 30 minutes or until a toothpick inserted in the center comes out clean.

Hard Tack Biscuits

These biscuits, made without baking powder or baking soda, became as hard as rocks. The cowboys softened them in coffee, stew or just plain water to make them edible.

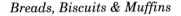

Buttermilk Raisin Muffins

2 EGGS, beaten
2 Tbsp. VEGETABLE OIL
1/2 tsp. BAKING SODA
1 cup BUTTERMILK or SOUR MILK
1 cup GRAHAM FLOUR
1 cup WHITE FLOUR
1/4 cup packed BROWN SUGAR
2 tsp. BAKING POWDER
1/2 tsp. SALT
1/2 cup RAISINS
1/4 cup chopped NUTS

Preheat oven to 450°. In a bowl, combine eggs and oil and stir. Dissolve baking soda in buttermilk and add to egg mixture. In a separate bowl, sift together graham and white flours, brown sugar, baking powder and salt. Stir raisins and nuts into dry ingredients. Combine wet and dry mixtures, stirring only enough to blend thoroughly. Pour into warm, well-greased muffin pans. Bake for 5 minutes. Reduce heat to 350° and continue baking for 10-15 minutes.

Hat History

John B. Stetson was the father of the western style cowboy hat. He began production of the "Boss of the Plains" hat in 1865. It came unformed and the cowboy could shape it to his personal taste.

Desserts

Rodeo Time!

The word "rodeo" is a Spanish word that means about the same as roundup, stampede, bucking contest, frontier days or western days.

The first rodeos were probably just a bunch of cowboys that got together to see who was the best rider and roper. In those days, you didn't have to pay anything to watch the fun and folks just sat in their wagons and buggies or maybe straddled the rail fence. In 1883, Pecos, Texas held the first rodeo where prizes were given to the riders. The money for the prizes now comes from the cowboys themselves, they pay to enter a contest, as well as from those who want to sit in the stadium and watch.

Rodeos, with their Western influence, have rapidly spread throughout the world. Boots, western shirts, Levi's and ten-gallon hats are in style in many places too. And for evening entertainment, there's the very popular "sport" of line dancing and square dancing.

Rodeo events include: bronc riding, bull dogging, calf roping, barrel racing, team roping, bull riding, chuck wagon racing, steer tying and horse racing. You'll also see rodeo clowns, who not only entertain the crowds, but help to ensure the safety of the rodeo participants.

Orange Oatmeal Cake

1 1/2 cups fresh ORANGE JUICE
1 cup ROLLED OATS
1/2 cup BUTTER
1 cup SUGAR
1/2 cup packed BROWN SUGAR
2 EGGS
1 tsp. VANILLA
1 3/4 cups FLOUR
1 tsp. BAKING POWDER
1 tsp. BAKING SODA
1/2 tsp. SALT
1/4 tsp. CINNAMON
1 1/2 Tbsp. grated ORANGE PEEL
1/2 cup chopped NUTS

Preheat oven to 350°. In a saucepan, boil orange juice and stir in oats. Mix well and set aside. In a bowl, cream together butter and sugars. Add eggs and vanilla, beating until fluffy. In a separate bowl, sift together flour, baking powder, baking soda, salt and cinnamon; slowly add dry ingredients and beat into creamed mixture. Stir in oat mixture until well blended. Stir in orange peel and nuts. Pour into a greased 13 x 9 pan and bake for 35 minutes. When cool, frost with ***Orange Butter Frosting.***

(Continued on next page)

Orange Oatmeal Cake
(Continued from previous page)

Orange Butter Frosting

1/2 cup packed BROWN SUGAR
1/4 cup BUTTER
1 1/3 Tbsp. grated ORANGE PEEL
1 Tbsp. fresh ORANGE JUICE
1 cup SHREDDED COCONUT
1/2 cup chopped NUTS

In a saucepan, combine brown sugar, butter, orange peel and orange juice. Bring to boil and cook 1 minute, stirring constantly. Stir in coconut and nuts. Set aside to cool.

Peachy Bread Pudding

4 cups sliced fresh PEACHES
1/2 cup firmly packed BROWN SUGAR
1/4 cup BUTTER
4 cups cubed DAY-OLD BREAD
1/4 cup SUGAR
1/4 tsp. CINNAMON

Preheat oven to 350°. Combine peaches and brown sugar in a 1 1/2-quart baking dish. Melt butter in a large saucepan; add bread cubes, sugar and cinnamon and toss together until cubes are well coated. Spread over fruit and bake for 25 minutes or until heated through.

Caramel Corn

3 Tbsp. BUTTER or MARGARINE
3/4 cup firmly packed BROWN SUGAR
1/3 cup PEANUTS
3 Tbsp. DARK CORN SYRUP
1/2 tsp. VANILLA
1/4 tsp. BAKING SODA
Dash of SALT
5 cups popped POPCORN

Put butter into an 8-cup glass bowl. Microwave on high for 30-45 seconds or until melted. Stir in brown sugar, peanuts and corn syrup. Microwave on high 3-4 minutes to soft-crack stage (when a drop of syrup separates into hard but not brittle threads when dipped into cold water). Stir in vanilla, baking soda and salt. Put popcorn in a large bowl. Pour caramel mixture over popcorn, stirring to coat. Microwave on high 1 minute and stir. Heat on high 1 minute longer and stir again. Cool for 30 minutes, stirring occasionally to break apart popcorn chunks.

The End of the Cattle Drives

Cattle drives were at their peak for only about 20 years, during the 1870s and 1880s, until the railroads rumbled across the country, taking away the cowboys' jobs.

Fancy Peach Fritters

1/3 cup SUGAR
1/2 cup MILK
1 EGG
2 Tbsp. VEGETABLE OIL
2 cups FLOUR
2 1/2 tsp. BAKING POWDER
1/2 tsp. SALT
1 can (15 oz.) SLICED CLING PEACHES, chopped
OIL for frying

In a bowl, stir together sugar, milk, egg and oil. In a separate bowl, combine flour, baking powder and salt. Add to liquid mixture. Stir lightly. Add peaches. Heat oil to 365° and drop batter carefully by tablespoon into oil. Fry until brown on both sides. Drain on paper towels. Dip fritters in *Glaze Icing* and place on a rack to cool.

Glaze Icing

2/3 cup POWDERED SUGAR   **3 Tbsp. BUTTER**
1/3 cup MILK   **1/2 tsp. VANILLA**

In a saucepan, combine powdered sugar, milk and butter. Bring to a boil, stirring constantly, over medium-high heat. Remove from heat. Stir in vanilla. Let glaze set for 5 minutes.

Blackberry Jam Cake

1 cup BUTTER	3 cups FLOUR
2 cups SUGAR	1 tsp. BAKING SODA
2 EGGS, beaten	Dash of SALT
1 cup SOUR CREAM or MILK	1 tsp. CINNAMON
1 cup BLACKBERRY JAM	1 tsp. NUTMEG

In a bowl, cream butter and sugar together until fluffy. Stir in eggs, sour cream and blackberry jam. Mix until well-blended. In a separate bowl, sift flour, baking soda, salt and spices together. Combine mixtures; beat with a wire whisk until smooth. Pour batter into a greased and floured Bundt or angel food cake pan. Bake at 350° for 45 minutes to 1 hour or until toothpick inserted in center comes out clean.

Ol' Time Ice Cream

3 EGGS, beaten	1 cup WHIPPED CREAM
1 1/2 cups MILK	1 Tbsp. VANILLA
3/4 cup SUGAR	

Cook eggs, milk and sugar in a double boiler, stirring frequently, until custard coats spoon; cool to 80°. Add whipped cream and vanilla. Pour mixture into the can of an ice cream freezer and freeze according to manufacturer's directions.

Makes 2 quarts.

Applesauce Nut Cake

2 1/2 cups FLOUR	3/4 cup BUTTER
1 tsp. BAKING SODA	1 1/4 cups SUGAR
1/2 tsp. SALT	2 EGGS
1 tsp. CINNAMON	1 tsp. VANILLA
1/2 tsp. MACE	1 1/2 cups UNSWEETENED
1/2 tsp. NUTMEG	APPLESAUCE
1/4 tsp. CLOVES	1 cup chopped NUTS

In a bowl, sift together flour, baking soda, salt and spices. In a separate bowl, cream together butter and sugar. Add eggs to creamed mixture, one at a time, beating well after each addition; add vanilla and stir well. Stir in dry ingredients, applesauce and chopped nuts. Mix well. Pour into a well-greased cake pan. Bake at 350° for 60-75 minutes. Cool before serving.

Rice Pudding

1/3 cup uncooked RICE	3 1/2 cups MILK
1/4 tsp. SALT	1/4 tsp. CINNAMON
1/4 cup SUGAR	1/2 tsp. VANILLA

In a bowl, mix all ingredients together and pour into a buttered baking dish. Bake at 300° for 2 1/2 hours. Stir once during baking.

Sweet Potato Pie

3-4 lg. SWEET POTATOES
1/2 cup BUTTER or MARGARINE, softened
2 cups SUGAR
4 EGGS, beaten
2 tsp. NUTMEG
1 tsp. MACE (optional)
1/2 tsp. SALT
1 can (13 oz.) EVAPORATED MILK
2 unbaked deep-dish PIE SHELLS

In a large saucepan, boil sweet potatoes until tender; drain in a colander. When cool, peel and place in a large bowl and mash. Add butter and sugar and stir well. Add eggs and stir until well-mixed. Add nutmeg, mace, salt and milk; mix well. Pour into pie shells. Bake pies at 425° for 20 minutes. Reduce temperature to 325° and bake for 30-45 minutes more or until knife inserted in center comes out clean.

Singing Cowboys

Did you know that cowboy songs are considered by some to be the true folk songs of America? Singing helped the cowboy with loneliness and soothed the herds of longhorn on the trail. It was so important for cowboys to be able to carry a tune that trail bosses didn't want to hire them if they couldn't sing!

Pumpkin Pudding

2 EGGS, lightly beaten
1 can (16 oz.) PUMPKIN
3/4 cup SUGAR
1/2 tsp. SALT
1 tsp. CINNAMON
1/2 tsp. GINGER
1/4 tsp. CLOVES or NUTMEG
1 2/3 cups EVAPORATED MILK
1/2 cup finely chopped WALNUTS
WHIPPED CREAM
CINNAMON

Preheat oven to 425°. In a bowl, combine eggs and pumpkin; stir until well-mixed. Add sugar, salt, cinnamon, ginger and cloves; blend together. Stir in evaporated milk and mix well. Pour mixture into a lightly-greased baking dish. Sprinkle top with nuts. Bake for 15 minutes. Reduce temperature to 350° and continue baking for an additional 45 minutes or until a toothpick inserted into center comes out clean. Cool and then cut into squares. Top each square with whipped cream and a dash of cinnamon.

Cowboy "Pie"

For an impromptu dessert, cowboy cooks would cook up a batch of rice and then add dried raisins or apricots. They called the resulting dish a pie!

Homemade Lemon Sponge Cake

2 1/4 cups FLOUR, sifted
1 1/2 cups SUGAR
1 Tbsp. BAKING POWDER
1 tsp. SALT
1/2 cup OIL
6 EGGS, separated

3/4 cup COLD WATER
2 tsp. LEMON JUICE
1/2 tsp. grated LEMON PEEL
1/2 tsp. CREAM OF TARTAR

Preheat oven to 325°. Sift together flour, sugar, baking powder and salt. Make a well in the dry ingredients; add oil, egg yolks, water, lemon juice and peel. Beat with electric mixer until smooth. In a separate bowl, add cream of tartar to egg whites. Beat until stiff peaks form. Gradually fold egg whites into yolk mixture until just blended. Pour batter into an ungreased tube pan. Bake for 70 minutes. Cool 5 minutes in pan then remove to cooling rack. Frost with *Fluffy Lemon Frosting*.

Fluffy Lemon Frosting

1/2 cup BUTTER, softened
Dash of SALT
4 cups POWDERED SUGAR, sifted
3 Tbsp. LEMON JUICE
2 tsp. LEMON PEEL

Combine butter and salt in a bowl and beat until smooth. Add a few tablespoons of powdered sugar to butter mixture and continue beating. Add remaining sugar alternately with lemon juice and peel. Continue beating until light and fluffy.

Index

If you love cookbooks, then you'll love these too!

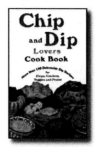

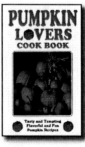

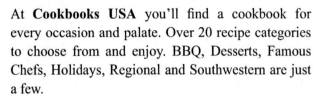